Cont(

The Total Emptiness Within

Alice D. Nate

This book is dedicated to my guru who always supported me. He gave me the confidence to follow my own path and to become a teacher.

Special thanks to my dear friend and colleague Martin who inspired me to write this book.

Special thanks to my students that showed very positive results and improvement in life after using this method.

Special thanks to my friend Tine for making the cover painting. I asked her to read the book and she came up with this stunning cover.

The

total

emptiness

within

is

a

view

on

life

a

concept

that

shows

you

that

true

contact

with

your

original

being

is

all

about

realizing

that

reality

as

we

perceive

it

is

completely

different

than

our

senses

tell

us

We

think

that

what

our

eyes

and

ears

see

and

hear

is

the

truth

because

we

sense

it

but

we

don't

realize

how

easily

we

can

be

fooled

Perception

is

controlled

by

the

ones

that

can

put

images

in

our

eyes

and

sounds

in

our

ears

If

we

can't

distinguish

the

difference

between

real

or

fake

anymore

how

do

we

find

the

truth?

What

if

our

perception

can

be

bent

SO

far

that

we

think

we

see

facts

but

what

if

these

facts

are

fiction?

What

if

reality

as

we

know

it

is

already

an

observation?

Words

fill

our

minds

images

fill

our

minds

sounds

fill

our

minds

Does

it

matter?

Yes

it

matters

It

materializes

the

reality

that

we

perceive

The

surreal

reality

is

perceived

from

our

spirit

that

observes

the

world

that

materializes

around

us

The

less

we

absorb

the

more

the

materialized

illusionary

reality

dissolves

and

the

real

reality

returns

That's

why

this

book

is

SO

empty

from

within

We

need

to

unravel

all

our

perceptions

from

the

mind

because

our

mind

and

the

body

are

part

of

the

materialized

observation

by

spirit

The

less

we

use

the

mind

the

more

we

return

to

the

original

point

of

observation

Our

spirit

looks

into

this

reality

through

our

body

and

mind

interface

Reality

can

easily

be

bent

by

the

masters

of

control

They

can

even

create

movie

or

game

like

situations

to

fool

our

perception

So

when

you

find

the

empty

page

look

at

it

for

a

while

and

let

the

true

meaning

of

emptiness

within

sink

in